John Kimber

The Trial of Captain John Kimber

for the murder of two female Negro slaves, on board the Recovery,

African slave ship - tried at the Admiralty Sessions, held at the Old Baily,

the 7th of June, 1792

John Kimber

The Trial of Captain John Kimber
*for the murder of two female Negro slaves, on board the Recovery, African slave
ship - tried at the Admiralty Sessions, held at the Old Baily, the 7th of June, 1792*

ISBN/EAN: 9783337198374

Printed in Europe, USA, Canada, Australia, Japan

Cover: Foto ©Suzi / pixelio.de

More available books at **www.hansebooks.com**

THE

TRIAL

OF

CAPTAIN JOHN KIMBER,

For Murder, &c.

THE

TRIAL

O F

CAPTAIN JOHN KIMBER,

F O R

THE MURDER

O F

TWO FEMALE NEGRO SLAVES,

ON BOARD THE

Recovery, African Slave Ship.

Tried at the ADMIRALTY SESSIONS, held at the OLD BAILY
the 7th of JUNE, 1792.

Before Sir JAMES MARRIOT, &c.

TAKEN IN SHORT HAND

By a STUDENT of the TEMPLE.

To which are added,

OBSERVATIONS on the above TRIAL.

L O N D O N:

INTRODUCTION.

ON a bufinefs which has fo long agitated the public mind as the Slave Trade, every thing that can be faid, muft in fome manner be interefting. The atrocity of that unnatural and abominable cuftom could not in any inftance have been more abundantly manifefted, than in the late decifion of a large majority in the Houfe of Commons.

Perhaps the procraftination of the fame important queftion, in a fuperior Houfe, may be productive of greater good than the people of England are aware of. Perhaps it may upon the next difcuffion lead to an immediate and total abolition of a cruel and inhuman traffic.

traffic. It cannot but be lamented that a perfonage of the firſt rank, who could have no other motive except that of love for un-controulable tyranny, ſhould become ſo ſtre-nuous an advocate for flavery. He has more than once expreſſed his ſentiments in public, and on the preſent occaſion ſeemed to have comported himſelf with an extraordinary de-gree of zeal, which whether it became the dignity of a P———— in ſuch a cauſe, we ſhall not take on us to determine, but leave it to the world to judge of the propriety of ſuch conduct.

Whatever the public opinion may be rela-tive to the proſecution carried on againſt Cap-tain Kimber, who has been (we ſuppoſe fair-ly) acquitted by an Engliſh Jury, it was e-vidently a neceſſary and a uſeful meaſure. It may afford a ſalutary leſſon to thoſe captains

of

of flave fhips, and mafters of flaves who
fhould hereafter attempt to commit fuch horrid outrages as he has been charged with:
and it may, from the circumftances here related, (for fuch barbarities have doubtlefs
been often practifed) fill the minds of men
univerfally with horror againft the prefent
fyftem: until tyranny fhall at length give
way to public opinion, and liberty and hap-
pinefs be reftored to human beings.

THE
TRIAL
OF
CAPTAIN JOHN KIMBER,
For Murder, &c.

THIS trial came on at the Admiralty Seffions held at the Old Baily, on Thurfday the 7th of June 1792; before Sir James Marriot, Judge Advocate of the Admiralty, Mr. Juftice Afhurft, and Mr. Baron Hotham.

The

The prifoner was indicted for having felo-
nioufly, wickedly, and with malice afore-
thought, beaten and tortured a female flave,
fo as to caufe her death : and he was again
indicted for having caufed the death of ano-
ther female flave.

Mr. Broderic on the fide of the profecution, firft opened the caufe.

Sir William Scott next ftated, that the prifoner, Captain Kimber, had commanded the
fhip RECOVERY, which traded in flaves from
the Coaft of Africa, to the Weft Indies : that
in 1791, he arrived in the river of Calabar,
whence he had, in fome time after, departed
with a cargo of flaves, among whom was
that negro girl, for whofe murder the prifoner now ftood indicted. She had been for
a confiderable time afflicted with a loathfome
diftem-

diftemper, and a lethargic complaint, which prevented her from eating, or mixing in any of thofe exercifes which the other flaves on board were accuftomed to practice. The prifoner had her punifhed for this fuppofed obftinacy; flogged her, and had her raifed up by pullies from the deck, fo that the tortures fhe endured, caufed her to languifh for a few days, until fhe died.

I fhall not, faid the learned Council, enter into a detail of circumftances, for that muft appear by the evidence which is to be laid before you Gentlemen of the Jury. Nor is it neceffary that I fhould make any obfervations on the heinoufnefs of this offence, as that is the province of the Court. And no doubt, your verdict will be given with that difcretion and impartiality, which has always been fhewn on fimilar occafions.

Mr.

Mr. Thomas Dowling was firſt called, and examined by Mr. Attorney General; he had been a ſurgeon on board the RECOVERY, the ſhip which the priſoner commanded: in the beginning of June, he had arrived in the river of Calabar, on the coaſt of Africa, where in the end of Auguſt they had com‑pleated their cargo of ſlaves. About the time of ſailing, he had under his care, a fe‑male ſlave, aged about fourteen or fifteen years, who had been afflicted with a virulent gonorhea, and lethargy, or drowſy complaint, of which latter ailment he could never learn the real cauſe. She was not then in a conva‑leſcent ſtate: but her diſeaſes were ſtationary, and bore every probable appearance of re‑covery. In this ſituation ſhe could not eat, as the other ſlaves did, nor join in any of their amuſements, at which the Captain was ſo irritated, that he uſed to flog her himſelf,

with

with a whip, the handle of which, was one foot long, and the lash two. About three weeks after they had sailed, he beat her in this manner with uncommon severity ; and on the 22d of December, perceiving her not to dance with the other negro women, he ordered a boy to bring a teakle, one end of which was fastened to the *mizen stay*, and the other to one of her hands, and by this she was lifted up from the deck, and remained suspended for about five minutes: and during that time, she was bounsed up and down, or in other words, lifted up, and let fall again, by the way, who had a hold of the teakle.

She was then taken down and suspended in the same manner by the other arm. She was next lifted up by one leg ; and afterwards by the other: until at last she was taken up for

the

the fifth time by both hands; and underwent
the fifth excruciating fufpenfion. The whole
time from the firft to the laft fufpenfion, this
witnefs faid might have been half an hour.
While fhe continued hung up by both hands,
the prifoner lafhed her inhumanly with his
whip: and when fhe was let down, he forced
her to walk without any affiftance down the
hatchway: this fhe was unable to do, having
got but two or three fteps, when fhe flipt all
the reft of the way.

When this witnefs next faw her fhe was
welted in feveral parts of the body, her hands
were fwelled in confequence of the hanging,
and her legs disfigured in a fhocking manner:
after this the witnefs faw her in convulfions,
had her brought on deck, and rubbed her with
volatile fpirits; but every remedy was ineffec-
tual: fhe languifhed away in this miferable.
ftate

ftate for three days, and on the third expired.

All this happened in the middle paffage a-
bout 200 leagues from Granada, whither the
RECOVERY with her cargo was bound. And
the witnefs was pofitive that the death of the
flave was occafioned by the ill treatment fhe
had received.

The witnefs was crofs-examined by Mr.
Pigott leading council for the prifoner.

Q. Has it been your undiviating opinion
that the girl died in confequence of the punifhment faid to have been inflicted on her.

A. It has.

Q. Was her death the fubject of no converfation at that time among the fhip's crew?

A. It was between me and Mr. Devereux;

and

and I heard the two boys Pearſon and Cruiſe ſpeak of it.

Q. How many men did the whole crew conſiſt of!

A. About ſix and twenty.

Q. At what time of the day did the fact happen which you have related?

A. Some time in the forenoon.

Q. You heard no converſation about it, except that between the two boys?

A. No.

Q. Are theſe boys now abſent?

A. I heard ſo, but cannot ſay.

Q. How many of the mariners do you think are now in this country?

A. I do not know. I mean to relate every fact which may go, as well to ſubvert my own evidence, as make againſt the priſoner.

Q. What time did you arrive at Granada?

A. On the 28th of October.

Q. Did you difclofe the death of this girl to any perfon at Granada?

A. No.

Q. How long were you there?

A. About a month.

Q. Did you go to the Cuftom-houfe while you were there?

A. I did.

Q. Did you keep a journal while you were on the middle paffage?

A. Yes: of whites, but not of blacks.

Q. Did you deliver in your journal?

A. Yes.

Q. And fwore to it?

A. The form of an oath was read to me,

by

by a perſon ſitting at a deſk : I took the book, and returned it without ſwearing.

Q. Did you ſign the journal as ſworn to it ?

A. Yes I did.

Here Mr. Pigott read his oath, which de-clared that his journal was a juſt and true one ; and the atteſted copy being handed to the witneſs, he declared, he did not recollect whether he had ſigned it or not.

Q. Is not that your name to the oath—and is it falſe or true ?

A. I do not recollect that I ſigned it.

Q. Is your bond diſcharged ?

A. Yes, I produced this copy at Briſtol, to have it diſcharged.

Q. Why did not the cauſe of the death of the negro girl appear in your journal?

A. The

A. The apprehenfions I had for my own fafety, while I failed with the prifoner, prevented me from relating it.

Q. Is it from difclofing a barbarous murder?

A. Yes; becaufe the prifoner and I had often quarrelled, and I might have been judged an improper evidence againft him.

Q. At what place did you quarrel?

A. At the river of Calabar.

Q. Did you not mutiny?

A. Never.

Q. Did you not ftrike the prifoner?

A. I did, after he had abufed and ftruck me on board his fhip.

Q. You collared and held him?

A. Yes, at the cabin door; when the firft

and

and fecond mate came and feized me, and by the prifoner's orders, I was put into irons, where I continued twenty-four hours; and I was afterwards excluded from the cabin, and obliged to mefs with the common men.

Q. Did you not tell a Mr. Jacks that you would be revenged on Captain Kimber?

A. No, I never faid fo.

Q. Did you not fay you would work his ruin?

A. Never, there is not fuch bafenefs in my nature. I never made a declaration of the kind to any perfon: but I faid I would advertife him for his treatment of me. After my arrival in Briftol about Chriftmas laft, I applied to Mr. Jacks, who was part owner of the RECOVERY, for my wages: he only paid me a part of them: I then complained

to

to him of Captain Kimber's treatment, but did not difclofe the murder.

Q. Did you not tell a Mr. Riddle that you would ruin Captain Kimber?

A. No: but I faid I would commence a fuit againft him for his fevere treatment of me, and that I would put myfelf under the protection of the firft king's fhip I met with. This converfation took place before we failed from Calabar.

Q. Did you never fay any thing to the prifoner's fervant?

A. No.

Q. Did you ever adminifter any mercury to the girl who died?

A. No: it was improper for her complaint.

Q. Can

Q. Can you pretend to fay that the fufpenfion of this girl, was intended as a punifhment?

A. I fhall not fay that; but it was obvi-
vious that it was a punifhment.

Q. Might not the Captain have had reafon to conclude that this fufpenfion was neceffary?

A. He might have had a motive, but I
did not know it: he never confulted any perfon in what he ufed to do; and he has often
interrupted me in the difcharge of my duty.

Q. In what part of the fhip did the fufpenfion take place?

A. On the awning deck.

Q. And when it happened in fo open and
confpicuous a fituation, as that it was impoffible it muft not have been feen by the fhip's
com-

company; why was it not a more general fubject of converfation.

A. I fuppofe it was, but I had not an opportunity of hearing it, except between Pearfon and Cruife.

Q. What was the caufe of your having at length difclofed this murder with which you now charge the prifoner?

A. I was folicited by Mr. Lloyd, a Banker at Birmingham, to give an account of the firing on the Town of Calabar; and from that relation, this account followed as a cafual circumftance. I told it to Mr. Wilberforce the day before he made his fpeech in the Houfe of Commons: but I never intended to profecute or appear in evidence againft Captain Kimber.

Q. So then this murder remained a fecret

until the day before Mr. Wilberforce made his Speech in the Houfe of Commons?

A. No: I told it to perfons in private.

Q. How often had you failed as a furgeon before this time?

A. That was my firft voyage, and it fhall be my laft.

The witnefs was re-examined by Mr. At-torney General, in order to account for fome of thofe circumftances which came out on his crofs examination, and might go to invali-date his teftimony.

He faid that he and the two boys were on the awning deck when the girl was fufpend-ed; that between this deck and the other part of the fhip there was a barricado about nine feet high, which prevented thofe perfons in the fore-part from feeing what was done abaft.

abaft. By this means many of the ſhip's crew,
who were on deck, might have remained
without ſeeing or knowing what was done to
the girl. And this might have been the cauſe
why the circumſtance had not been generally
ſpoken of on board. When I gave in my
journal, ſaid the witneſs, at Grenada, I wiſhed
to omit every mention of the Negro Girl,
from the apprehenſions I was under for my
ſafety, not knowing what the priſoner might
have done ; I therefore wiſhed to evade the
oath which is made on thoſe occaſions, and
accordingly when the officer tendered it to me
I took the book from him, and returned it
without kiſſing it : he was fitting at a desk and
did not ſee me.

The witneſs requeſted that the Court would
examine the log book, where they ſhould ſee
that this death, which he omitted in his jour-

D   nal

nal, did really happen. And the prifoner he faid had told him that a journal was a mere matter of form.

He faid alfo that when Mr. Loyd and Mr. Wilberforce had examined him relative to the firing upon the Town of Calabar, the latter gentleman queftioned him as to the treatment of the flaves on board the fhips, and it was upon that occafion he told him the circumftance of the murder for which the prifoner was now indicted; without having had the remoteft intention of profecuting him. And he moreover obferved that outrages of that nature were fo common on board the flave fhips, that they were looked upon with as much indifference as any trifling occurrence; their frequency had rendered them familiar.

Stephen

Stephen Devereux, the next witnefs on the fide of the profecution, was examined by Mr, Soliciter General.

He depofed, that he had failed to the coaft of Guinea in the *Wafp*, from whence after he arrived there, he changed as third mate into the RECOVERY, which failed from Africa on the firft of September; he remembered the decafed Negro Girl very well: after he had been ten days on board, he faw Captain Kimber endeavouring to ftraiten her knees which were bent and contracted, and afterwards flogging her with a whip. While I was ftanding faid the witnefs, on the ftarboard fide of the quarter deck, I faw the girl running up by the gun takle, which was faftened by a block to the mizen ftay: fhe was fufpended by one of her arms, and continued raifed above the deck for four or five minutes;

fhe

fhe was let down, and lifted up again by the
other arm, and Pearfon the boy who held the
takle jerked the fall : In this fituation the boys
were endeavouring to make her legs ftrait. She
was taken up the third time by one leg, and
the fourth time by the other ; after which fhe
was fuffered to remain on the deck for fome
time. In this fituation with her head droop-
ing between her knees, Captain Kimber, who
was prefent during the whole of her torture,
lifted her up, gave her a flap on the face, and
faid *the bitch is fulky* : and then again endeavoured to ftraiten the contraction in the knees,
with the intention of inflicting punifhment
on her. The fifth and laft time fhe was lifted up by both hands, but her feet touched the
deck ; and in this pofture the prifoner flogged her feverely. When fhe was about
going down the hatchway he would not fuffer
any body to affift her, but faid *the bitch is fulky*

fhe

she must find her own way. After she had got down two or three steps with great struggling and difficulty, she slipt along the rest of the ladder. All this happened in the morning.

I saw her the next day, and helped her up on deck: she was in a very filthy and shocking condition, quite weak and feeble, her body was covered with whales and bruises; she was not put down along with the other women; but was suffered to languish until she died, on the third day after the suspension.

Q. What other persons belonging to the ship's company were in sight of this business, besides the Captain, the Surgeon, and yourself?

A. The man at the wheel, and one or two more.

He

He was cross-examined by Mr. Sylvester.

Q. Was you not dancing with the women, at the time this bufinefs was going forward?

A. I was looking at the women dancing; but when the girl was fuffering the punifhment, they attended more to it, than to any thing elfe.

Q Were there any, and what other perfons with you at the time?

A. I don't know.

Q. Could you attempt to fay, that it was by way of punifhment that the prifoner endeavoured to ftraiten the girl's knees?

A. I know of no other motive he could have.

Q. Why did you not mention this bufinefs at Grenada, on your arrival there?

A. I

A. I did not wifh to concern myfelf about
it, particularly as Captain Kimber had behaved to me as a friend. Befides, every fea-
man on board muft have heard of, or known
it: and the Surgeon and I have often talked
of it fince.

Q. Did you ever give any information of
this affair, till you were fent for to London?

A..No.

Q. And when you appeared before the Ma-
giftrate in London, did you not fay that you
were ignorant of the caufe of the girl's
death?

A. I did, for the reafon I already mentioned, being delicate of doing any thing
that might endanger the prifoner's life. But
I am now certain, that if fhe had not been
punifhed in the manner fhe was, fhe would
have lived, and been fit for market.

[Here

[Here Mr. Sylvefter read the depofition of this witnefs, which was taken before Sir Sampfon Wright, at Bow-ftreet, about two months ago, when the prifoner at the Bar was brought before him, charged with the murder for which he was now tried : in this depofition the prefent witnefs Devereux had ftated, that he did not believe the girl died in confequence of the punifhment inflicted on her: a contrary teftimony to which he now gave to the Court.]

Q. Did you venture to take any of your fhip's crew along with you, to give evidence of this bufinefs you now fwear to?

A. No, they were all taken up at Briftol, and fent away.

Q. Are there not fome of them now in London?

A. I do not know.

Q. Were

Q. Were you not difmiffed your fhip as firft mate for mutiny, while on the Coaft of Africa ?

A. No : I did not mutiny.

O. Were you not charged with having mutined, and tried before fix Captains ?

A. The charge againft me was, giving the lie to the Captain.

(Here Mr. Sylvefter read the charges againft him wherin he was ftated to be a pernicious, dangerous, and troublefome fellow, and accordingly was turned away from the Ship: but there was no fpecific offence mentioned.)

On his re-examination by Mr. Solicitor General, he faid that he had mentioned the Murder of the flave to feveral perfons, before he came to give evidence of the firing upon the town of Calabar : and to a Gentleman at

E   Briftol,

Briftol, after Kimber had been brought up to town. He did not know where the reft of the Crew had been.

Captain Kimber he faid was one of thofe who formed the Court, that tried him on the Coaft of Africa; and that he afterwards took him into his fhip and treated him in a friendly manner.

Thefe two were the only witneffes who appeared on the fide of the profecution.

Mr. Walter Jacks was firft called on behalf of the prifoner, and examined by Mr. Pigott.

He faid he was a merchant in Briftol, and had a fhare in the RECOVERY, which the prifoner commanded. He knew the prifoner fix years, for three or four of which he had
been

been in his Service: and he was always fatisfied with his conduct: for he was good to the
fhip's company. Mr. Dowling, who had been
Surgeon to the fhip attended this witnefs at
Briftol to demand the ballance of his wages,
which had been due to him.

At that time he complained that Captain
Kimber had engaged to allow him two pri-
vileged Slaves, and that afterwards he would
give him but one. The witnefs told him it
was impoffible he could have double privilege,
as one Slave was all that was ever given to
the furgeon of that fhip: but in paying him his
wages, he gave him fterling money inftead of
currency; as a fmall compenfation for the
hardfhips he faid he fuftained.

On the tenth of laft January, after Dowling had received his wages, and thanked the

E 2   witnefs;

witnefs; he told him that Captain Kimber
was a rafcal and a cheat, and that he would
ruin him if it was in his power. And im-
mediately after the prifoner had been taken
into cuftody, thefe words occurred to the
witnefs.

Thomas Lawer lived at Birmingham, he
had frequent converfations with Dowling
about the flave trade, who faid, he had frequent quarrels with Captain Kimber, in one
of which he ftruck him, and was afterwards
put in irons, turned out of the cabin, and
obliged to eat falt provifions with the fore-
maft men.

The Captain allowed him but one privi-
leged flave, and had behaved very ill towards
him, for which he was determined to be revenged. Thefe words he often ufed.

Benja-

Benjamin Riddle was examined by Mr. Morgan.

He faid he had been Surgeon on board the *Thomas,* which was on the coaft of Africa, at the fame time with the RECOVERY. There he heard Dowling fay, that he had been maltreated by Captain Kimber, and that he would ruin him if poffible: that he had a memorandum in his poffeffion, which he could produce againft him, when he came home. The witnefs afked to fee the paper, but Dowling would not fhew it. This was a fober deliberate converfation, and Dowling thought he was fpeaking to a friend.

After this, the witnefs heard Captain Kimber fay, that Dowling's conduct was fo bad, he could not keep him : he ufed to bleed, when it was evidently dangerous, and commit

mit other improprieties in his profeſſional line.

The witneſs alſo knew Devereux to have been diſmiſſed from the *Waſp* for mutiny.

Mr. Dowling was again called, and aſked whether it was true, that he had told Mr. Jacks, Lawer, and Riddle, that he would be revenged of, and ruin Captain Kimber if he could. He perſiſted in his former aſſertion, and declared that he had never ſaid any ſuch thing. He told the Court, that if they would indulge him with a hearing, he ſhould clear every matter to their ſatisfaction; but having proceeded in a deſultory manner, he was prevented from ſpeaking.

Captain Thomas Philips was examined by Mr. Knowles.

He

He depofed, that he was on the Coaft of Africa when the prifoner was there. Deve- reux had been turned out of the *Wafp* for mutiny, and had acknowledged the charges againft him to be true: and the witnefs knew him to be a bad man.

There were, he faid, on board Captain Kimber's fhip, great quantities of oranges, which Dowling ufed to give to the flaves. The witnefs told him often, that fruits were bad for them ; that they would caufe the flux, which difeafe, it appeared, the deceafed girl was afflicted with : and he knew, for twenty years he had been in that climate, fuch dif- eafes carry off perfons in the fpace of two days.

The witnefs knew the prifoner fince he was at fchool, and he never heard any thing in- jurious

jurious to his character, until the prefent charge was preferred againft him: He was always humane and good natured.

Thomas Lancafter was a mate belonging to the *Wafp*. He faid, that Devereux had admitted the charges made againft him : and all the fhip's company looked on him as a dangerous fellow. After he had been turned out of the fhip, he remained on fhore for two months ; and if Captain Kimber had not taken him under his protection, it would be impoffible to tell what fhould become of him.

Devereux was again called, and queftioned, as to the truth of what had been faid againft him : and he declared it was as falfe as that *one* was *two*.

He

He was proceeding to make a defence, when the Jury faid they were all fatisfied from what had appeared to them; that there was no credit to be given to the two witneffes on the fide of the profecution, and therefore found the prifoner

NOT GUILTY.

It ftill remains for us to make a few obfervations on the above extraordinary trial. Nothing that may now be faid can in any manner affect Captain Kimber; as he has been acquitted, and cannot be tried a fecond time for the fame offence.

We fhall not declare what impreffions we lie under as to the guilt or innocence of Capt. Kimber; but lay before the public a few points, from which they may draw fuch con-

F   clufions

clufions as their feelings and reafon fhall
dictate.

And firft we fhall afk, why was there not
fuch a defence fet up by Captain Kimber, as
could, in the minds of the people, have acquitted him of the horrid act which was
fworn againft him? Did he bring forward a
fingle witnefs to contradict the charges of
his accufers? What became of all the feamen
and fervants on board his fhip, who were in
England at the time he was apprehended,
and who might have been brought into Court
to declare at once that the prifoner did not
commit murder; without having recourfe to
the miferable fhift of proving perjury againft
Mr. Dowling and Devereux, in points that
had nothing to do with the profecution?
Were none of the RECOVERY's crew to be
found, or was Captain Kimber afraid that
they

they would have all conspired against his life?

One of the witnesses on the side of the prosecution said, that all the crew were taken up at Briſtol, and ſent out of the way. The event has given us no reaſon to doubt the truth of this aſſertion.

As to Mr. Dowling's not having diſcloſed the murder when he came on ſhore, nor keeping a complete journal, theſe are cir-cumſtances which thoſe perſons who know any thing of ſhips in general or the African ſlave trade, will pay no attention to. Jour-nals, which are conſidered mere matters of form, are generally imperfect, and the bar-barous treatment of ſlaves on board the ſhips is ſo frequent, as to be looked upon with in-difference. Perhaps Mr. Dowling, perhaps the

the whole crew might have conceived that the killing of a flave on board a fhip was an offence not punifhable by law.

As there was no other evidence to fupport the fecond indictment, than what fupported the firft, the Jury alfo acquitted the prifoner on it.

The trial lafted near five hours. His Royal Highnefs the Duke of Clarence was prefent the whole time, and appeared from his looks and geftures, to be particularly interefted, in favour of the man who was accufed of having murdered a flave.

F I N I S.